About the Author

As a child Jane would clearly see people from the spiritual world. This was not accepted as Jane was born into a Catholic family so she tried to suppress and conceal her ability. It became stronger throughout her military career and motherhood, until she eventually decided to embrace and develop her gift. Jane feels honoured to see the true beauty, love and light in her work as a channel writer for the spiritual world.

Dedication

I have been taught there is nothing to fear in life. Fear is manifested from within and it doesn't need to exist if you take control. This is the hardest discipline of all but can be achieved.

Thank you, Eddie, for listening to my panic stricken telephone calls but most of all for sharing your wisdom, support and love. I feel truly blessed to have met you on my journey. Thank you. X

Jane Lee

MYSTIC MOMENTS
IN
LOVE AND
LIGHT

A CIP catalogue record for this title is available from the British Library.

ISBN 9781785542756 (Paperback)
ISBN 9781785542763 (Hardback)
ISBN 9781785542770 (E-Book)

www.austinmacauley.com

First Published (2016)
Austin Macauley Publishers Ltd.
25 Canada Square
Canary Wharf
London
E14 5LQ

Contents

What is Important?

To cherish the experience of life
To be humbled by the love, kindness and acceptance of others.
The warmth and acceptance of the passer-by
The stranger who will risk his life.
People, animals, nature, clean air, swaying of the trees
And the insects, including the humble bumble bee
Everything that has a soul and enables
The soul to evolve,
That's what's important.
The lessons we learn on our paths
The heart wrenching truths of despair
The highs, the lows
The unconditional love we give and receive
The teachings we share
And words of kindness
But also the moments of silence
Just being there
That's what's important.

Shoes

Whose shoes are you wearing?
Whose footprints are you imitating?
Whose style and personality are you intrigued by?
Are you clumping around
Or gracefully gliding?
Whose shoes are you wearing?
How about a pair of shoes for you
Just you
A snug fit
A style all of your own
A shade that matches your individuality.
Maybe not everyone's cup of tea
But yes
Your cup of tea.
To finally find a pair that suits you
Your beliefs and values
Your outlook and sunny disposition.
A comfort
Almost like slippers
For these are your shoes
This is your path
And it suits
Yes suits you
Now it's time to follow your path
A path so divine
It's unquestionable to falter off
For this is your journey
A journey wearing the right shoes.

A Coat

A garment of protection
It shelters you from the wind and the rain
It protects your body and undergarments.
Take that coat away and you may become cold, wet and
weary.
You have to search for shelter
You may become frightened if the weather becomes
aggressive and threatening.
Someone offers you your coat back
How do you feel?
Happy content, secure and safe
In control and dare I say, slightly empowered and confident.
It's not much in life to ask for.
See the power of giving
A small gesture
A humble sacrifice
To give the most important gift to another
A coat
Which turned into shelter?
Which turned into self-worth?
Never forget that.
Next time you go to make a few bob on the internet for
yourself
What could those unwanted belongings give and create for
another?
Endless really.

Dogs

A fellow companion
The kindest friend of all
The one who understands when I need to be left alone
The one who knows when one has been left alone long enough.
The excitement and anticipation of the greeting
The soul who takes nothing and expects nothing.
A gentle soul who gives unconditional
Love, time and pleasure
Truly gives.
So what am I so enamoured with?
My truest friend
My ally
My companion and soul mate
Yes my beloved four-legged canine
My dog.

Guidance

When all around seems to be crumbling
You look for guidance
Ask for guidance
Send out that thought and miraculously it will appear
Maybe not straight away
But trust and it will appear.
Guidance, what does this mean?
It means staying on your true path
Not being swayed from your true inner intentions.
You all have a path you have to walk
It's the guidance from your loved ones
Who will ensure you don't falter.
It really is as simple as that
Sending out a thought for help, support and guidance.
A guidance to help not only oneself
But all who walk the path
At different times with you.
A guidance to help others
When they are struggling with the demands life throws at you.
A reassuring hand
A safety net so they know
If they are to fall
You will make sure they are caught.
We are all interlinked
By asking for help, the universal law
Will reach out and in return
You will help another.

Happiness

Happiness, a feeling of contentment
And joyous sensation within
At present not a care or a worry in the world
At present that is.
Enjoy the moment
Don't question it or analyse it.
Before too long you have thought yourself out of this happiness.
We all experience happiness throughout our lives
But don't always embrace the moment.
You have weathered many storms
Consisting of many emotions, heartache, anxiety,
Low moods and yes for many ill health
So why not just flow with it and enjoy this unexplainable happiness.
For you deserve it
Be happy
Don't complicate things
For life is already made more complicated by others
Just enjoy
You have earned it.

Inferior

Always feeling inferior to another
Whether this be academically, financially
Or simply, not as good?
Hush the hurt
Hush the silent tears you weep internally so no one can see.
Quiet yourself
Feel the tremble of electricity
That vibrant, powerful energy within
Ignited and desperate to come out
You are powerful – a power house
To help so many others
Ever thought those feelings of inferiority
Many others are feeling too?
Hidden like yours from the outside world
These feelings of inferiority
Will enable you to empathise with others
Connect to others.
Those who haven't experienced these emotions
Can't help the diversity of people throughout our land.
Feel blessed that you can put these feelings to good use
Be thankful for every emotion you experience.
We are all different, perfectly unique
Embrace every feeling and put to good use
Feelings are given to us as a gift from above
To be able to empathise and heal others.

No More

No more words, no more worries
No more rushing, no more hurries
No more.
For today the skies are blue
And the air is clean
So no more worries
No more worries.
For worries are a waste of energy
And energy we all crave
So no more worries
I repeat no more worries.

Pitter Patter

Pitter patter, pitter patter
I hear the sound of tiny feet
Tiny feet that belong to a shining soul.
A soul who is already developed
Strong and wise
So don't underestimate the child's side.
This child will grow to be kind and unique
If nurtured, loved and shown what to be a fleet.
Never overlook the tiny feet
For these are the future of our world
A future of devastation or one or true bliss
All down to the future of
These tiny feet.

Rhythm

Lose yourself to the beat
Express your body freely
Let the sound of the music run wild
Through your veins
Exploring the inner vibration of your body
Hitting and ricocheting off every inner organ.
Feel the electricity generated within
Allow your body the freedom
No thoughts
Just sense, feel the rhythm
Escapism
Just in the present moment
Just rhythm
Nothing more, nothing less
Just your body free with the beat
FREEDOM
Allow yourself this regularly
For there is no better medicine
That solves the anxieties of our busy worlds.
Throughout your lifetime one must
Learn the art of self-healing and a coping mechanism
To enjoy and experience this journey to the full.
Simply listen, escape and feel
Nothing more, nothing less
Listen to the rhythm.

Time to Play

Time to play
Really play, do something that you really enjoy
Immerse yourself in creativity
Run around a football pitch
Swing from the trees
Splash in the waves
Just go and play
Be care free
And enjoy the play.
Silence the mind and immerse yourself
In whatever it is that makes you happy.
Escape from the world
Even if just for today
Free yourself from the chains
You have locked yourself in
If just for today.
Play is part of life
It makes life bearable
You played as a child
Whether you had much or very little.
A child knew how to play
Why is it then as we grow
We lose the art of imagination
And the freedom to enjoy simplicity?
Nobody un-taught you
So if only for today
Take yourself away
And remember how much fun you had.
I hear so many say
Well that's because I hadn't got all these responsibilities of …
The list is endless
So I will reply
Can you not see then just how important it is

To find time to play?

Mirror

Mirror, mirror on the wall
Who is the fairest of them all?
Shallow how one compares another to oneself
Appearances, possessions, bank balances.
That's how we compare one another's success
Shocking.
So many on the outside
Appear to have it all
Take another look
For some that is all they possess.
They don't feel the value a loved one receives
The warmth of a smile from deep within.
The unconditional love children and animals are so natural at
giving
The feeling of completeness and contentment.
Sad how so many long to be part of something so special
Another or a pack.
Humans like all animals require love
Without this
One has very little
In fact one has nothing.
So who is the fairest of them all?
The beautiful princess with all the wealth
Locked in her own tower she has built
Or
The peasant who lives among the poor surrounded by loved
ones?

Love

Everybody needs a little love
Whether that be the love of another or
Love of life
The air on one's face
The love of the mountains, nature itself
That deep sense of contentment within.
There are so many sensations, words and expressions
That we call love.
When you see that rainbow pure, radiant
And an element of magic
It holds love.
Love is all around us
In the air we breathe in and exhale out
We are all connected through love
For every breath we inhale and exhale
Is shared by many
A never ending chain of energy
Electricity formatting through all.
Thoughts are so powerful
Sent with love they are truly uplifting to all.
Words of encouragement and positivity
These all equal love.
Stop when you acknowledge a dark thought or self-creating
fear
Change it into a lighter thought and see
The impact on your life and others
For love is the most powerful
Gift we hold and therefore
The responsibility is to share it with others.
The gift of love is in all our hands and hearts
Not to be wasted this opportunity.
A world of lightness all within our hands
Make that choice.

Slow Down

Life is so precious,
Consists of very little time
You haven't seen a friend's child for a while
Suddenly they are an adolescent
Where did that time go?
Nothing stands still for time
Everything is maturing and developing at great knots.
But we can stand still
We can silence ourselves just for a little while
To reflect on what is important
And what is zapping our energy which needn't.
Stop if just for today
And let those nagging insignificant problems go
Concentrate on what is important
Truly important
What holds dear to your heart?
Your burden you carry upon your shoulders
Will lighten and life will become more joyous again.
Time is of the essence
Enjoy each day
Embrace life
And decide what you can do to lighten your load.

A Rose

A beautiful rose
Starts off as a tender tightly closed bud
Nurtured by the soil, wind and air.
Gradually teased out by the loving elements of nature
Curious by the warmth and light of the sun.
Gradually feeling brave and secure in one's self
To start to open up.
Each day, little by little,
With love
The rose starts to really bloom
Until one day
The rose stands with silent confidence within
That this is who they are.
Now everyone can see who they are
For they have learnt
The art of self-acceptance
And embrace everything about themselves.
Yes, even the imperfections
For once, we know our self-worth
And all we have achieved
The sense of contentment, appreciation and how fortunate we
are.
We project that love of life and serenity to all.

Freedom

The raw elements upon one's face
The wind, the rain, the temperature of the air
Beautiful.
Not a care in the world
Just for that moment
No thoughts of anything.
Just that moment of silence
Contentment and freedom.
Bliss
Allowing yourself to be you
No pretence
No conforming to society's rules and expectations
Just you, the here, the now
Heaven.
Allow yourself to roam freely in the wild with Mother Nature
A park, a garden
Close to nature
All you need is a few seconds each day
To ignite that fire of freedom within.
An opportunity to ignite your soul
Let it breathe in all the wonderful
Organic elements
That's freedom
True freedom
A freedom so free it doesn't impact on another
But will fire up your soul
To fulfil what you are here for
Your journey, your choice.
As you have learnt the art of freedom.

Philosophy

One person's perception on a topic
Put into a multitude of words
Sounding important, educated and very clever.
Really!
Why can't one try speaking with honesty
Simplicity, truth and integrity.
A language and simplicity all can understand
For simple language, gestures and kindness speak volumes.
Words are often not needed in certain situations,
A knowing look
A heartfelt energy exchanged from one to another,
So powerful.
Silence is gold in the harsh reality of the busy world
Peace is even more precious
Often the fewer words spoken
The greater the impact.
Never try to ridicule another by speaking
In unfamiliar words
Of self-importance
Be humble, kind and gracious
And learn when words are truly needed
Or silence is more powerful.

A Bench

A tatty wooden bench
Exposed to the elements of the weather
Unkempt, looks dirty, tired and worn out.
Still standing strong though
Might look old, but still bumbling along.
Many a story that bench has heard
Many a tale to tell another.
If one would listen to the older generation
A wealth of knowledge
A lifetime of experiences
So much could be learnt
And unnecessary mistakes need not be repeated
If only one would look
Beyond the exterior.

Hush Little One Don't You Cry

Hush
Don't silence
But just hush
What is it that ignites?
The tinge of sadness within
The creation of loss and anguish, deep physically within.
The tired, dull feeling upon one's forehead
Don't silence it
Scream, shout, and let it all out
Or just
Let it be.
Let these feelings run their course
Watch them, explore them and gradually they will become more subtle.
The turmoil of emotions will ease
So hush
Let it be
For you are evolving and healing in the process.
Don't ignore how you feel
But tentatively watch
Here today, gone tomorrow
Nothing can stand in your way.

Angel

In the arms of the angels
They are everywhere
We are truly surrounded by the presence and love
Of the angels.
The showering of blissful happiness
The content warmth one feels within
The excitement of a child
And innocence of an infant.
All these blissful emotions, sensations and more
Unexplainable love and acceptance.
We have all experienced these things, some only for a glimpse
Others have been fortunate and can reminisce.
But all have had that stir of unexplainable bliss within
Something has stirred that sprinkle of energy within.
Admiring nature
Breathless by a piece of art or abstract
Animals
Fresh air
The wind on ones face
The heat of the sun on your body
Life itself.
For every breath you inhale and exhale is not just you
But divine
For angels are present
They are everywhere.

Beautiful

Beautiful roaming hills
Picturesque scenery, waterfalls
Glaciers upon the mountain tops.
So much beauty
The beauty of an animal
A strong powerful athletic stallion
The beauty of the rain running down of the window sill.
Look a little closer
Not with one's eyes
But with one's senses, thoughts and feelings.
Feel the beauty of within
We've all met a person who is so beautiful within
Breath-taking how much beauty
A person can possess within
Much more than any living creature on the exterior
For with time, the strong athletic stallion
Becomes old and withered
As all living species naturally evolve with time.
The true beauty within is timeless
Never fades or ages
For beautiful energy
Is pure light and eternal
So look within, not just at yourself
But others, too.

Choice

So many wounded souls
Where does one begin?
But we must begin
Each and every one of us is here
Born here to make a difference
Simple gestures
A kind word
A warm smile
To acknowledge another
Can heal so many
Laughter can result in tears of joy
As tears are a healthy emotion.
Tears of joy
Or tears of sorrow
All release tension within one's soul
We have become so suppressed over time
Not allowing ourselves to express our emotions and thoughts
Taught from such an early age
How to conform to society
No wonder there is so much ill health and mental disease.
Created once again by ourselves
By this I mean man
Man has so much to answer for
But with a little love and kindness
Man can change
For no one is chained to routine
For there is a thing called CHOICE.
Through choice and experiences
Man can change
The world can become a better place and will through time
CHOICE
The willingness to change and make the right decisions.
Nobody said this earth plane was for the light hearted

The contrary
It's for the full hearted.

Bricks

Bricks layered in synchronisation
One on top of another
Perfectly placed
Manually or mechanically placed.
A thought will come your way
Place the first brick down firmly
For the foundation of your ideas
Are most important.
Ask yourself your intention?
Who will benefit and why?
If honourable and heartfelt
The foundation will be strong,
The bricks will not crumble
For truth and integrity are solid foundations
And will stand the test of time.
Continue to place the bricks
With confidence and self-assurance
For it will only occur to you
Once you reach the top
How marvellous the journey has been
And the value of the lessons upon your path.
Once the wall is finally secure
For all to see
Enjoy but never forget the foundations
You set out with
How strong your values are and must remain.

Waves

There's something truly beautiful about the crashing waves
Upon the beach
The energy and emotion as the wave hits the shore.
Once the wave hits and releases the energy
It becomes subdued, content and subtle
For the anger and pent up storm has been expressed
Nowhere to hide for it is out in the air
For all the elements surrounding to see.
Some of the wave returns to the sea
But not as angry
Some of the water remains on the shore and dissolves away.
Each time the waves come crashing in
Little by little the waves begin to settle.
Eventually there is a beautiful green and blue ocean
The sun is reflecting off the sea
And the glisten of the ocean is breath-taking.
The ocean consists of such great depth
A depth that not all will discover
But for now it is victorious
For the wave is calm
Until the next gathering of storm clouds
Appear to unsettle the tide
But for now and only now really
Exists
Is calm.

The Trunk of a Tree

Have you ever looked at the trunk of a tree
Cut through the middle
Chopped down?
It tells a story
Circle upon circle
Life circles.
Some smooth and uncomplicated
Another a little rockier
But all go round in circles.
So many circles of life
Precious each and every one.
Everyone has a story to tell
All need to be listened to
To freely express, share and be heard.
So many talk
But how many listen?
If you learnt the art of listening
You too could be so knowledgeable
Like the hundred year old oak tree
And gain all that knowledge.
To listen is a gift
For so many have fallen like the
Chopped down tree and can no longer grow.
If one doesn't learn the art of listening
The branches become no more,
The leaves wither and the buds die
For you can't bud and bloom
Without learning
From the old oak tree.

Travel

Travel is a privilege
So many trap themselves in the material consumption
Convincing them it's best for the children and family members.
Some decry the warriors who pursue their dreams as selfish
How could you leave your family?
Travel to the other side of the world
Really
If one was truthful, by saying this
There in itself is the suppressed child
Who would desperately love the freedom of travel?
With travel comes freedom to explore
New avenues, people and cultures
With this comes a true appreciation of all one has
And how little others have.
A world of simplicity
Where if one asks oneself the truth
We need very little
But have become blighted with consumption
Of useless and wasteful materials,
At once made us happy and shortly leave us a nothing feeling.
True happiness comes from life experiences.
Look at life with humble and non-judgmental eyes
To pass comment and listen to views
But not to judge
Every culture is different
But not as unique as each and every one of us.
Travel is a gift we can all do
Many confine themselves to the mundane,
So be free and travel.

Healing

As a wound always heals
There are stages of each event
Each natural event takes the time
Our bodies will allow it.
For you can't rush the process
An acceptance is required
Small baby steps
Until one day the wound has healed.
You didn't notice it healing
One day it had gone
So had the pain, discomfort and aching
All gone.
The memory was still there
The body and soul never allows
The tiny fragmentation of memory to dissolve
For it is embedded deep within.
A precious flicker of light
Embedded deep within
For all those beautiful memories,
Some good, some indifferent become part of us.
I hear so many worry about losing the memory of a loved one
That loved one is part of you
A tiny fragment of light
Held deep within your soul
The memories, let me assure you, will be going nowhere.

I'm Here

As you walk by in life
I'm here
As life becomes too much
I'm here
When you hear the joyous laughter of others
And tremble of joy is felt within
I feel also.
When worries of financial burdens and the material world
Becomes too consuming
I'm here.
Strange how wonderful occurrences keep happening
I couldn't pay the bill
A letter arrives with a back payment
That's because I'm here.
You never walk the path of life alone
Although so many feel alone and unloved.
Too many can't fulfil the journey
As darkness infiltrates their weak energy
And life is taken
From oneself
Not another
But oneself
So sad
If only they could of felt, sensed or listened
They would have realised
I was always here.

Rush

Rush, rush, rush
No time like the present
Things happen for a reason
One can't rush the process
As those who have lost a loved one, will vouch for this
You can't rush the time of the wounded
You can't predict the future
No one can.
We all have control of our destiny
But one thing is for sure
We all have the choice.
One should never blame another for one's outcome.
The final decision is yours
You have to make that decision.
No one else
But you.
Yes you can listen to advice
How about listening to your self
What do you think?
We all know the difference between right and wrong
And how our decisions can impact on another.
When you're making a decision
It is up to you to be accountable for your actions
Your intentions.
You can blame others for the outcome
If all doesn't go to plan
But it takes a bigger
Courageous person
To be accountable for
Your life, your destiny and your decisions.
This earth plane is your schooling
It's how the schooling goes
To how successful your time has been.

Never blame another
For this is your time.
Use the time wisely
And you can become king or queen of your throne.
A throne to help others nurture and guide
But ultimately their decisions are theirs
Like yours are yours.

Rain

Beautiful rain
Glorious rain
Felt upon one's face
Feel the freshness
The slight chill
That brings you alive.
Rain
Pitter patter, the sound of delicate
Rhythmic sounds
In perfect unison
The moist soil
Nourished and rich
Exploring different shades and tones.
Rain
Flowers vibrantly exploding with rich colours
Almost rejoicing with anticipation and hunger.
Rain beautiful glorious rain
Enjoy
For some aren't blessed
With the seasons we take for granted
As though
It is our automatic right
For it is not
It is the right of Mother Nature
Not for us to
Tamper with as, one is.
Rain enjoy
Never take for granted or presume it is our right.

Strength

You were my tower when all around had crumbled
You were my strength when all had disappeared.
You were my rock when I wept
And my angel when I had slumped to the depths
You picked me up when I felt so alone
You brushed me down when I had fallen
You gave me hope
When all seemed so dark
You ignited that inner spark.
For you I am so thankful
For all I have truly learnt
That no untoward can come near me
With all that you have taught.
I thank you for your strength
That you so willingly shared
And now it is my time to care.

Thank You

Thank you, such a precious word, not said enough throughout our time.
So important for folk to be thanked
As to say thank you a little often would create a greater will to strive to help others.
A wanting
A desire.
To thank one, creates more light and as we know light equals love.
Love has the ability to open so many doors,
Doors of good fortune.
It is how we say thank you that really matters.
If said from the heart it is truly very powerful.
An emotion that will touch another's soul.
For we all know and feel when someone truly means it.
Never use the word unless it's from your soul
Otherwise it becomes useless energy, meaningless and worthless.
To say thank you and to mean it is precious.
THANK YOU.

I Can't

There is nothing in life you cannot over come
Or learn from
Disastrous actions from one another
Can always be overcome.
The destruction, pollution and overcast
Shadows that taint our lives
Can all be learnt from.
Often worldwide disasters created by man
Cannot be replicated
By this I mean
The anguish, pain and horror experienced deep within.
The depth of despair physically, emotionally and spiritually
No further depth can be made
For one has experienced the anguish
Beyond.
But through time, healing and the simplicity of nature
Perhaps the song of a bird
You allow yourself to return
Return to, at first exist
Then breathe
Then see
But now you see with clarity and wisdom that surrounds you.
You have a choice
To see with negativity and scepticism
Or
See with hope and aspirations
To make a difference help and teach others
That man-made monstrosities of destruction is not the way ahead
We must learn from these horrendous occurrences
Which enable us to see through the smog
How beautiful life really is and how
Precious we truly all are.

How Long Will I Love You?

Once the exchange of heartfelt love is felt
It can never be parted
People part throughout their journeys
But true love never dissolves
Never dissipates.
For once the energy of two souls unite
They are inseparable
Entwined within one another.
You will go on to meet many others
But true love can never die
For the captivation of the two are embedded.
Beautiful really
The same as one departing the earth plane
Before the other.
The connection of the two souls
Who have truly loved and cared for one another
Cannot be parted.
Physically yes but not mentally, spiritually
Or from the soul.
As two souls touch one another's energy
This is for life, eternity
So true love is therefore eternal.

Looking Glass

Look through the looking glass
What does one see?
Hundreds upon hundreds of lost souls
Overcome by materialism of the world
Hold on
I see one who is different
One that's not the norm
One who's not part of the flock
It's you
You are unique
Special and see the world through
Not only the looking glass
But what life's all about
A life that is to be valued
A life that is fun if you allow it to be,
One of immense adventures
Obstacles and challenges.
A world of emotions and complex vibrations
All entwined with one another
This life is amazing
At times heart breaking too
But it's what you learn on your journey
And how you develop into you that matters.
Grasp every moment
Live for the here and now and cherish
Every soul you come into contact with
For they are part of you
And you will become part of them.
Nourish, grow and never condemn another
For you are condemning yourself.

Nature

Snowflakes falling on a winter's day
Pure and honest
Pure in color, pure in intention.
See how the flakes settle upon the ground
Uniformed, precise, with honesty and good intention.
One waiting behind another
Waiting for one's turn.
No pushing or shoving
Each flake knows where to settle
And just how important that one's job is.
No need to look at what the other flake has or is going to do
For they are equal
As we are all equal.
Universal law – beautiful
Especially with nature,
It doesn't fight the elements but succumbs to nature.
Nature always has a habit of rebalancing itself.
Over time there will be calmness but
Now all must weather the storms for Mother Nature
Needs to rebalance herself
To protect us all
Especially the vulnerable.
At times this may appear cruel
But one has to look beyond and ask what the intention is?
The intention is for all to live in harmony
With equality and equilibrium within the air.
Fresh air and atmospheric is to be shared upon all
For there is no discrimination or lack of acceptance
Upon all living species,
Yes including man with Mother Nature.

Reflection

Reflection of oneself
Look carefully
Look within
See the soul
Fighting to be heard.
So often our inner self wants to give one the answer
To a worry, a problem, an inner desire
But instead of listening to our inner self
We opt to listen to another.
Another with greater knowledge
Experience, Material wealth
Whatever it is we see that makes us believe
Another is better than us.
Quite shallow really
Don't you think?
The way one puts another on a pedestal
If one puts another on a pedestal is it because
We secretly desire
Another to fall off?
Is this for our own gratification?
Never put another on a pedestal
For we are all equal.
Yes we have different
Talents, beliefs, materialism
But it truly doesn't matter
What really matters is the ability to look within
See that bright soul within
Made of pure light and love.
It will never let you down
Just simple honesty
And always the right answer
There is no risk of being let down
For your soul is pure.

Go on take a risk next time and ask.

Sad

So sad
How one can self destruct
A self-loathing, nothing another
Who tries to comfort and support can help.
For the self-loathing is so engraved,
Engraved since childhood
So much anger and hurt
They don't know how to express.
Afraid they could hurt another
Much easier to self harm
For if you inflict hurt on yourself
Surely you're not hurting anyone else?
Wrong
For those around you feel your pain
Especially the young
Who can't quite understand
But yes they feel.
The impact of hurting yourself
With over indulgent of so many different kinds
Whether it is
Food, alcohol, nicotine, drugs, different diets, over exercising,
Is so blatant to a child
But so complex to an adult.
If one hurts themselves in what they think in silence
Think again
A child or a loved one feels powerless
Powerless to help.
How do you feel when you self sabotage
Not at the time
But afterwards?
Think
There is always a solution
Only available when one asks.

Roaming Hills

Look at the roaming green hills
The landscape is breath-taking
Similar to life, beautiful.
Green pastures, new beginnings all the time
Crevasses hidden away
Tripping over
Mud on your path
Unbeknown to you some unexpected rocks that often get in the way.
That's the beauty of life
The highs, the lows, the mundane moments
Nothing ever stays the same.
As the roaming hills of nature
Appear beautiful and smooth from the distance
But once up close they appear so different.
The same as people
Should you always look from a far?
Or perhaps become that little closer.
Perhaps you'll find that rose upon the thorns
Perhaps not.
Never lose the ability to challenge yourself
Among the beauty of all
The excitement within
The inner child to explore new adventures.
Life is challenging
It's meant to be challenging
Never shy away from a new challenge
Just because you are scared of failure.
Failure is not trying
Failure is being hidden behind that closed door
And looking from the distance at the beauty
But never truly feeling the beauty
That's failure.

Daisy Chain

Remember making daisy chains as a child?
The time spent
Lovingly placing one daisy delicately through another stem.
The time, patience and love you put into that important procedure
A necklace of love
Or tiara of great importance
If you had the time
You would wear and give to another.
The simple pleasure that was created
Even more important the time you spent with another
Or for another.
That gift you made for another or yourself
Was made with love
Not financial love
But pure love from within
The excitement and appreciation
You whole heartedly knew that person would feel
No doubt
For they would receive with gratitude and excitement of their gifts
Gifts from the heart are priceless
But mean the world.

A Bin

A bin is where you throw your rubbish
It gets thrown away in a land fill site
Under all the rubble
What one often isn't aware of, is it takes years to disintegrate
Some rubbish never dissolves
For it's not bio degradable.
Like our rubbish and the things we hide
Out of sight from others
Kept hidden in cupboards or buried in land fills
You can't hide the inner turmoils
Well not from yourself
As they keep reappearing
And exposing themselves
Often stronger.
Before you throw your rubbish away
Make sure you deal with it properly
Then you can lay it to rest
Among the rubble
But this time for good.

Earth Beneath our Feet

Take your shoes and socks off
Make the time
To stand upon the grass
What do you feel?
Try again
Feel the roar of the earth
And the crisp, cold, slightly damp grass
Upon your toes.
Feel the stability and safety of our land
Feels a little shaky at the moment.
The earth fighting to survive, grow and develop
But we as humans keep stunting her growth
Not allowing her to bloom into her full potential
For if we did
The land would be full of
Plantation, fruition and the sound of wildlife everywhere.
When was the last time you heard
The sound of a cricket?
Perhaps as a child if you were fortunate enough?
Enjoy Mother Nature in all her fine glory
For nothing can be taken for granted
As the ones we hold dear to our heart
And the ones we don't
Evolve all the time.
Some to pastures green
Others to another time
But for now enjoy for everything and everyone
Is evolving.

Life is Good

You're on a roll at the moment with life
Everything feels good, even, balanced.
One has nothing to moan about
Life is good.
Embrace this moment
Don't look for a worry or a concern.
Maybe when life is mundane and balanced
You have the time to reflect and absorb.
Not create an unwanted fear or scenario
But enjoy
Oh yes life is to be enjoyed
So many forget this
It's OK to be content and in a good place.
Never feel guilt for these precious moments.
For you have earned them
The law of nature
Everything naturally evolves
Every minute of every day passes
As does life.
Enjoy the moment
The here and now
Embrace.

I'm Proud

Have I ever told you just how proud I am of you?
Well I am
I'm so proud of the way you are
How you perceive the world with openness
A desire to see good in all
Even when others have been cruel.
The way in which you conduct yourself
Remaining non-judgmental to all
You have your own standards for yourself
But never expect the same for others.
A kind heart
An open mind
A joyous smile
Always willing to help another
But refusing to put upon another.
You are priceless, more than any gem
You are you
Oh yes, did I ever tell you how proud I am of you?
I'm proud of you.

Spring

Spring is in the air
Smell the sweet aromas for they are so subtle
Feel the freshness upon your face
It's glorious
So pure and innocent
The new life
Soon to be upon us.
So exciting and unassuming this time of year
So much to see and value
All within our vision.
Welcome for all to share
Glorious
Nature doesn't discriminate
It is for all to share and enjoy.
All it requires is your acknowledgment
So, go on
Stop and stare.
It costs nothing
But enriches the soul
Creativity within the mind
And enlightenment within.
The true value of our existence is to embrace our universe
Not to bypass it.
For if one does
You have missed your vocation and reason for being here.
So please, stop and stare
Amazing what one will notice
All for the taking, for all to share.

Squirrel

Squirrels here squirrels there
Squirrels everywhere
The grey squirrel clambering up the tree
Still unsure of its destiny.
Surrounded by folk
But still untrusting
Once a creature with so many habitats
But now one of so small.
Seems like there are so many
But actually so few
Just the lack of square footage
They have been forced into.
An unsure time for the squirrel
Nuts becoming few
Homes becoming sparer
Enjoy the humble squirrel
Watch and observe
For time is of the essence for so many
Of our furry friends.
Once we would call them vermin
But as time stands still for no one
They are now called our furry friends.
Educate the children and every time
You see a living creature
Stop and stare.
For stare you must
For such precious moments
Must be retained, for these times move quickly
As our furry friends' habitats will become few.

Tears

Hush little one
Don't you cry
For I am by your side
Wipe away tears of sadness
By this I mean, I am still alive.
The shell of my body no longer exists
But my soul and spirit
Are always here.
For I cannot die for I am truly alive
Our time will come when we will be reunited as spirit and
souls
But until that time
Don't weep
Don't cry for as I have said
I am very much alive.
As you will find, as all will find
On the other side.
For one must not fear these words
For these words are truly comforting
As I shout from the rooftops
I AM ALIVE AND CAN NEVER DIE
For we are all energy
And energy is alive.

Hold On

Hold on
Always hold on to what is dear to you
Memories
Keepsakes
Senses and smells that remind you of another.
These things are so valuable
Priceless
And create emotions within
Very powerful.
So hold on, hold on
And remember one day
All these senses, emotions and unexplainable feelings
Will once more be yours
Hold on.

I'm Dying

I'm dying
We are all dying
Every second of every minute of the day
Our shells or bodies are aging
One cell splits and divides in the incorrect way
We become ill.
One tragic accident after another
Souls are released from their bodies
Sad, but true.
We are all dying, just at different rates
Some may be unfortunate not to experience
Their first breath
The breath of life.
Others will suffer the turmoil of ill health and live
What seems to the bewildered forever.
So yes we are all dying
But wait a minute
Surely you don't believe this is it?
This is merely schooling
A school for all to learn
At different rates
But one you will attend
And eventually you will learn
For no one escapes the lessons of life.
Yes your body is dying,
Surely you don't believe you are
Do you?
How can that be?
It's impossible for you to die
Yes the shell of you
But not the true you.
Thought provoking, you'll just have to wait and see.

Work

Work, work, work
There must be time to play
A balance of both is required to enjoy
The simplicity and beauty of this world
Without yin and yang
Light and dark
Laughter and sorrow
We can't appreciate what one holds so dear
In front of our eyes.
The blossoming tree, developing child and
Ageing grandparent
Nothing should go unnoticed
Nothing does go unnoticed
Your hard work is acknowledged
Although you may feel indifferent
All is noticed.
Are you noticing all around?
Yes you must strive to do your best and achieve
But not at the expense
Of those you hold dear to your heart
Or dare I say what planetarium occurrences are developing
Right before all our eyes.
Balance
Life's all about balance
Do we crash and burn with self destruction
Consuming too much?
Where one will eventually tip the scales or
Reflect now and react?
Slow down and enjoy the moment
Yesterday is in the past
Today is NOW
Tomorrow may or may not exist
Enjoy.

A Canary

A small yellow canary bird
Tweeting away
Joyous in song, joyous in air
Happy and content in the finery and safety of the cage
Knowing I can chirp away with contentment
For nothing will come to the canary's harm.
As the canary is surrounded with steel finery
Trapped and safe within the bars
No need to venture
For all is fine within my finery
No need to look beyond
For all is safe and calm in my surroundings.
No need to explore and develop
Or even change my chirping
For I am content with my lot.
I have surrounded myself in safety
I am provided for by others
I dare not want for more
For I have everything.
I have a home, I am slave to
I have food I need not work for
I can chirp about nothing for I have experienced nothing
But chirp I will to others
For I am a product of so many
Living a life of simplicity
But unable to breathe the elements of nature
Feel the fire, hungry to express
My inner desires
For I am a conformist
A canary.

I'm Sorry

I'm sorry
Can be the hardest words of all
If genuinely meant and felt
Can help another move on and empower.
 People who have been really hurt
Just desperately want to hear those words.
All I wanted was, I'm sorry
That would have meant the world to me
I could have moved on.
Don't get me wrong I'm still hurting
But now I can carry on.
All from the words, I'm sorry.
Often when one has lost another
People are scared what to say
Especially if the circumstances are tragic.
Much easier to cross the road
Or send a message letting them know you are here.
How about being there
Open for the other to be comforted.
Give that person the choice of opening up and healing
Or remaining closed
The opportunity to be comforted.
Never be scared to look another in the eye
And say, I'm sorry.
Yes this can be uncomfortable
But also a chance to help another.
If nothing else
Your bravery
Will have touched another's soul.

Time

Time is of the essence as we all know
Time
What is this?
For all that matters is the here and now
Yesterday has gone
As will today
You can't change the past
But you can influence the future.
If others won't forgive you
You must learn the art of self forgiveness
Without this art
You cannot progress
Progression and learning is what we are all here for.
Silence one's mind, calm your soul
Forget yesterday's events
For today only truly matters.
It is the progression, learning and acknowledgement
Of one's faults that matters.
If you have acknowledged
Then all is forgiven
And yesterday is in another time.
Self forgiveness, so important
Forgive, move on and strive to be better
And kinder to others.

A Child's Love

A Child's love is pure
Feel the way that little person holds your hand
The gentle soft skin that hasn't be exposed to the elements of
life
Not a care in the world
Yes they might skip across the path
Sing a little song
Blissfully happy in their world
Watch
Watch the children next time.
It's funny, it will make you laugh
That's what the divine intended for us
That freedom, honesty and openness to explore our
surroundings
Express ourselves freely
But also to know what's right and wrong
That's what all of us really desire out of life!
But how we complicate life
It could be so simple
It takes a brave adult to return to these qualities
For what would others think and say?
Who cares!
It's your life
This is your time
To learn and explore this planet
So many live in the footsteps of others
You have your own path and your own foot prints
Make them count.

A Feather

A white feather floating from the sky
Watch the feather gracefully floating
Rocking calmly, rhythmically swaying
From side to side
Touching the earth so gently
Tenderly and yes lovingly.
There's not an ounce of aggression
Anger or turmoil
Pure simple grace.
A grace and charm to gently touch
A soul on its path
That desperately needs it.
Needs the comfort of knowing
There is something
More beautiful and tangible,
Than just this.
A message for a loved one
From a loved one.
So many signs of purity and communication
Surround us on a daily basis.
So, so much love surrounds each and every one of us.
Some aware
Some unaware
But it doesn't matter
For the presence of our loved ones never discriminate.
Through time scientists will discover
And learn more about greater energies
But until that day
It's up to us all to make our own decisions.
For some this is second nature, for other's nonsense
But rest assured each and every one of us will be rewarded
For our kindness and love to others
As you will discover.

Have Faith in Yourself

To have faith in yourself
One of the most difficult things to do
You can't learn this
It can't be obtained by practise
It has to be simply done.
Not for the faint hearted
But for the true warrior.
Faith
Faith in yourself
Takes many a lifetime and beyond
But if you are serious about achieving this
There is no going back
For this will be the new you
A content, fulfilled, surreal you.
One that never doubts one's actions
For the intention will always be pure
The intention will always be of helping others
A complete selfless act.
For to have faith in yourself
Will affect so many.
Every action of every day
Will be for universal benefit.
As we have said before
To hold true faith in oneself
Is not for the faint hearted
But for the true courageous warrior.
A warrior who does not just desire
To make a difference
But has been sent from above
To make a difference.

Growth

Trees swaying side by side
In unison
Perfect synchronization
For nature is perfect
Every bud beautifully formed,
Some smaller and not so defined as others
But all here to fulfil their job.
To bloom in full flower
To us humans this is the most beautiful and breath-taking moment.
What about the hard work, growth and fight to grow
Through all the harsh winter elements.
That's not to go unnoticed
The process before the mighty bloom.
Always stop and think
Not what another has but,
How did they get there?
What is that person's story?
There has to be sacrifice and hard work
Often a touch of sadness to allow the strength and determination to arrive at full bloom.
It's the process before that makes us the person we are.
For this chapter builds the strength within and fuels the fire.
One must keep the fire burning within
Lit at all times.
So warmth and desire can be given to another.
Everyone has a fire to light within.
It's up to you how bright it shines
Never just see the materialism another person has
Stop and look beneath
Are they warm?
Do they shine brightly?
If so then take some of that energy

That burns brightly and learn from them.

Dreams

Dreams
Everyone should have a dream
An inner passion and desire to strive for that dream.
Dreams do come true
There is nothing that one can't
Obtain and achieve if the intention is to benefit all.
An idea will come your way
When least expected and all will become clear
Crystal clear.
A synchronised chain of events will occur
Appears coincidental
But as we are all aware there is no
Such thing as a coincidence
Suddenly things flow
Everything is moving in the right direction
Contacts are made
Things are really happening.
This can't be happening to me
Things like this don't happen to people like me
Yes they do
If the dream is to put something
Back into society and truly help another
The dream will come true.
Dreams can come true
Always hold that dream within
And one day perhaps it will become a reality.

Courage

We all have courage deep within
Courage is a desire, flare, light energy
Waiting to spark free.
So many dampen and suppress this emotion and energy
Held deep within.
Thankfully there are many that will let loose
This energy out into the world.
For when courage is set free
It ignites another's self-worth, passion and integrity
To do what is right.
There have been many martyrs throughout our time
That has allowed courage to speak out for many
Sometimes at the expense of one's self
But never at the expense of all.
On the contrary
This courage has saved the lives of millions
Allowed free speech
Human rights
Inhumane acts on animals, children and all living species.
Protection and love for all,
Without that first courageous person
Where would we be today?
Perhaps the dinosaur age?
You pick
Never deny yourself that courageous moment
If to help another or to better oneself for the good of all.
You have no right to dampen that fire within
For that fire is for all.
STOP HIDING especially if it will benefit another.

Sorrow

Emotions in turmoil
A feeling of hurt and distress within
A sick churning sensation
Within one's stomach.
A sense of loss
A deep sorrow and sadness deep within
No one can help
A feeling of distress, vulnerability and loneliness.
Stomach churning nausea and a physical desire
To empty the soul.
We do listen; we do witness and feel your despair
And it brings us great sorrow and sadness.
Each and every one of you will experience
This unbearable sensation and emotions
For nobody escapes the loss of
Losing a loved one,
Whether it be a friend, child, parent, animal
Someone of true importance within one's life.
All we can say is the physical and emotional hurt will
With time ease.
That little piece of loss
Won't ever go away
But time is a great healer.
If only you knew the other emotions and sensations
That lay ahead of you
The joy, the laughter, the love and the light
An over controlling sense of pure bliss, contentment and
joyousness
Once again unable to put into words.
For one's loss on the earth plane
Creates sadness but on our side it creates the above.
A time for true celebration
A celebration for the time that person experienced on earth

However little or long the time.
For now our loved one has returned
Returned home to where all belong
Whether you believe this or not
You will all find out
Nothing to fear, nothing to dread
Pure harmony, love, light and a sense of belonging
You're finally home.

Sunshine

To truly appreciate the warmth on your skin
The beautiful blue skies
The flowers daring to open one's petals
You need to have experienced the chill in the air
The storm so aggressive
One has to find shelter
To make one's self feel safe.
If you have weathered all the storms and elements of life
The truly ugly situations often put upon us?
Then you enjoy that sunshine
You embrace every moment
Ignite the inner child within and celebrate.
For you deserve that sunshine
For you have conquered and weathered the storm.

Words

Sticks and stones may break my bones
But words will never hurt me.
WRONG!
Words if allowed can break the fragile
Wound the child
Suppress the growth of an adult
Reduce the innocent to tears.
Words can speak louder than actions
Frightening really the responsibility
We hold on the tip of our tongues.
Do we allow the words to roam freely?
Without a care in the world
Or do we stop and think a little before
We blurt out what is on our minds.
Devastation or enlightenment
Demoralisation or empowerment
Hurt or happiness?
So important to always think of another
Or how you might feel
For some are more fragile and sensitive than others.
Make or break that bone?
For if you decide to make
That person will become stronger in time
To help build another and another.
Don't break, always strive to make.

To Sleep

Escapism from the world
Where do you go whilst asleep?
Not a care in the world
Once you are asleep
Where do you go?
Many travel between the worlds
The moon, the stars, astral.
It doesn't really matter where you go
It's the sensation you feel within
No restrictions, no inhibitions
Weightless without a care or worry in the world.
Free to roam where the heart desires
Freedom, beautiful
It's a shame so many can't remember
The experience when one returns back to the here and now.
Or is it?
Maybe our subconscious won't allow us or maybe our minds
But our souls know the truth
That's what keeps us on the straight and narrow.
If we truly believed this was it
Mankind and all living species would lose the art of caring
If there was no caring in the world
There would be no consideration for one another
And earth would become a very bleak place
Full of darkness
But it doesn't
Our planet consists of huge amounts of light and kindness.
Why is this?
Because all know deep within
This isn't it
There is a beautiful kingdom waiting for all
Accepts all and loves all
Just a heartbeat away.

The Sound of Nature

Listen to the sound of nature
The rustling of the leaves upon the ground
The wind whistling
The birds cheeping
Listen
What else can you hear?
Really hear
The busy roar of the car speeding down the road
Something so important
They are willing to threaten the life of another.
What else can you hear?
The constant stream of traffic
Congesting our roads
Fuelling anxiety
For nothing stands still for
The importance of work, hustle and bustle
Which fuels other's energies
To join in with the rush.
I hear in the distance a plane
Oh yes polluting our skies
So not only satisfied with polluting
The earth but also our skies.
Wait a minute
I hear the car doors slamming
The windows opening and clattering
Where has my sound of nature gone?
I can no longer hear the sound of the wind
And the sweet song of the birds
The hedgehog rustling in the leaves
STOP!
What is going on?
Take yourself away from the rat race
Breathe the fresh air in

Look, listen and sense all around you.
Back to basics
Or what's the point?

Ocean

The ocean so deep
Each level of the ocean
Consists of many shades
An array of colours
Some without names.
Look how the light reflects and glistens
On the top layers.
As we go deeper
The light appears to disappear
But nobody truly knows the colours so deep
For they are invisible to the human eye.
For man cannot explore pass a certain depth
But the depths as we know go further.
Perhaps a whole kingdom hidden away
With more colours and array of lights
Man has never seen
Or could even vocalise for words haven't been invented to
describe.
Some things in life will never be explained
Some kept secret to protect the worrier.
But one thing is sure
The truth and beauty of unexplainable occurrences
Eventually rise to the surface.
For truth, honesty, love and light
Cannot be hidden for ever
For it's the universal law.

Hurt

The feeling of hurt is so individual to everyone
Almost indescribable
A deep sadness
Hurt held within
A sorrow so deep
A lonely child in despair
Not knowing where to go or who to turn to
A lost soul.
All this emotion and turmoil is no good for anyone.
The self-destruction and self-loathing,
Often created because it is easier to hurt one's self
Than to be open to the world and allow others
To see that inner, vulnerable child in desperate
Need for love and support.
Sad isn't it how we allow ourselves to reach
Such low depths.
Let me tell you a secret
There is always someone to help you,
All you have to do is ask.
Simple – try it
For this is the law of nature
There is so much love and support around you,
You just have to send out that thought.
It's called the power of love which is held throughout our universe.
It's OK to feel like this for we have to experience everything.
It is what you do with these feelings.
Spread them to others or empathise with others in their hour of need.
Only you will know, for you have all the answers.

Marriage/Commitment

Marriage
Some say one is married to their job
Married to their hobbies
Married to another
What does this word mean?
Surely not just the vows spoken on one day?
Marriage is an ability to see the others point of view.
Listen to the drones of repeated stories, worries and concerns
Repeated over and over again.
Putting another before your own needs
Sharing the highs as well as the lows
Wiping away the stray tears,
The reassuring of another's worries
Basically being there.
Not because of vows spoken on one day
But because you care and want to share
That's marriage.
Once again you share, not because of spoken words
For a legal obligation
But because you care.
Marriage is a word that symbolises a commitment
Of two souls who choose to share the present moment of time
Whether they be married on paper
Or simply married to one another.

Life

In sickness and health
The cycle of life
We go through many cycles throughout life
One of conquering all
One of defeat and despair
One of remorse
One of true bliss
One of sadness and one of triumphant.
We experience so much while we are here
But it takes the brave warrior to stop,
Acknowledge the different stages and reflect how much we have learned.
It takes the even braver, to teach others
By this I don't mean lecture others
But plant a seed of hope and light
Another option on a circumstance
Not to be blinkered.
As there are always several choices to one situation
And many different outcomes.
One must be there for all scenarios
As I have already mentioned
In sickness and health
To truly learn and understand the cycles of life.

Patience

Patience is a virtue
I never really understood this
But now I do
Everything arrives at the right time
You can work and strive hard
But occurrences in life will present
Themselves to you when you are ready.
Often you're not expecting anything to occur and then
You hardly have time to absorb the realities of all
Going on around you.
This works best for so many
For some could not cope any other way.
Always strive to do your best
But remember things occur always at the right time
For a reason.
Not for one to waste time analysing over
Simply embrace.
Embrace every obstacle thrown your way
For nothing in life will be presented to you
That you cannot cope with.
Enjoy the challenges on your path
Just try not to force and definitely don't rush
For the foolish miss the lessons upon the journey
And the wise enjoy the ride
Knowing it is the journey
That teaches you the wisdom
Not the final destiny
Patience.

Plantation

Miles upon miles of tiny trees spread across the land
In their tiny small brown encasements.
Does this look natural?
Does this resemble nature?
I fear not.
It will take many years before the up and coming trees
Play a role on our environment
Cleanse the air, filter the smog.
Yes the smog which is to become
Far worse than ones' imagination can picture.
For many not all, will not blossom into adulthood
Don't think by planting man made multi-quadruple trees
This is nature.
For many lucky ones
You still envisage the rarity of Mother Nature
And the scattering of the seeds of multicoloured flowers.
The smell of sweet fern of the trees
For some of our young
They will never get to experience or envisage the beauty,
Earth once had
But through pictures from books or Kindles.
There has to be a stop button
If not for the love of ourselves
Then for the love of our children and their children.
That's not even to mention the impact on the animals, insects,
flora and fauna
It takes the brave to act
And the ignorant to ignore
Which are you to be?

A Fresh Start

Today and every day
Is a Fresh start.
Yesterday's, worries are in another time
And no longer exist
As tomorrow may never arrive
For today IS NOW
Live in the moment and strive to be the best you can.
By this I mean really be aware of others
Laugh, be joyous
But never at the expense of another
Be kind not because you feel you should
But because you want to
This is you.
The pure energy hidden within
Be accountable for your actions and thoughts
You can't be responsible for another's
But you certainly can for yours.
If you lead a life of simplicity
By this I mean
Basic human kindness
To help not hinder another's progress
You will notice
Life becomes so much more enjoyable and humbling.
A journey of self-discovery
With eyes open wide and fulfilment.

A Tattoo

A tattoo, originally a tribal tradition
But now for many a trend or fashion
One feels often, not always obliged to follow.
For many are individual and feel this is an expression or
creativity
But for many, with time, a regret.
An impulsive occurrence to fit in with others.
Does it really matter?
Not really.
For it's what's hidden beneath our armour that is so precious.
The spirit and true person within.
For this is what we should decorate our outer garments with.
The true us.
Not the one that conforms
Or often behaves in such an erratic hurtful and selfish way to
others
So not to conform.
Very complex, us humans
Maybe we should allow the world to see
Our inner selves shine through.
Brightly
Lovingly and courageously.
Wouldn't that be a statement?
To be your true self
Not for the faint hearted
For with bravery
Often comes ridicule and unpleasantness
But thank goodness
Many throughout history have taken that leap of faith
A faith that has resulted in helping so many.

Friendship

A partnership and belonging to another
An unexplainable respect and loyalty
A sixth sense about what the other is feeling
And a compassion to help and truly want
To make everything better.
A protective natural instinct to at times nurture
A desire to make another laugh
Really chuckle
To see things often differently
But to be open to the other's view
Most of all not to be judgmental.
Be honest if asked for your opinion
But respect you are two different individuals.
To find a friend in life
Is a gift from above
Thank you.

Rainbow

Red, yellow, pink, green, purple, orange and blue.
I can see a rainbow, see a rainbow, see a rainbow too.
Within each and every one of us consists a rainbow.
Red - The passion and fire if controlled and nurtured can truly become creative. Fire desires ambitions in others as well as one's self.
Yellow – bright, honest and full of vitality and cheerful intention. Unassuming but very powerful.
Pink – Love, the powerhouse of the universe without this most precious energy there would be no need to strive for humans, animals and all living species. All can't live without the flicker of love or one will lose all colour and the inner rainbow will become no more.
Green – Pastures new, adventures but an inner calmness, reassurance and knowing of one's path. Pure love.
Purple – The wisdom of knowing you are right and an unexplainable wisdom within. Born with this gift to serve others. Powerful and to be used in goodness for all.
Orange – Wise, tribal, powerful but unassuming. What you see in boldness doesn't express the humbleness within. Not often appreciated but happy to be bypassed.
Blue – Healing, beautiful, energetic and pure. Blue surrounds us all everywhere.
The sky, the ocean and the energy naked to the eye of so many. For we are constantly being healed from one situation to the next.
Every one of us consists of a complex rainbow full of emotions, expressions and hurts.
But let me assure you,
You are all beautiful unique rainbows
You just haven't realised it yet.

True Friendship

Another that has your best interest at heart
Will be loyal to the end.
Maybe not always agree with you and yes maybe at times
Will challenge you
Not because they want confrontation
But because they want you to see both sides.
A desire to help, not carry you along your path
Knowing there will always be a presence by your side.
Often not physically but a thought away
As you think of another
The other will be thinking of you.
A true friend synchronises with your energy
Will always know when friendship and support is needed.
That is not to say, you expect your friend to mind read
For you as a friend also must be humble, honest and open
To receive the support so many crave for.
For to be part of friendship is allowing and telling another
Of your difficulties.
Also being open and non-judgmental to receive,
Truly knowing your best interests come first.
Friendship
So valuable and so often taken for liberty
Never take a true friend for granted.

Yell

The freedom to yell
Wouldn't that be great?
Really yell
Let those inhibitions and issues out
Yell.
The freedom to express yourself
So many have forgotten how
Are almost scared to
If I started yelling,
Maybe I wouldn't be able to stop.
Easier to contain and self sabotage
Can't upset or hurt anyone else
If I maintain control all the time.
But you are
For we are all unique energies
And can feel the destruction and turmoil within one another.
Spreading our energies to all
For we are all connected.
It is our responsibility
To face our inner hurts, issues and deal with them
Nobody has the right to inflict and pass onto another.
As the cycle of life and history matters go from one
generation to another
Often the young born into beliefs and behaviour
They don't even understand.
If there's one thing positive you can do on this earth plane
And really make a difference
Then yell.
Deal with the hurts
Deal with the feelings of hatred
Despair and anxiety
Free yourself and others from those chains.
If just for today let it all go

Stick your head in a pillow and YELL!

Confusion

So many feel like you
Confused by life
Asking what one's purpose is
An inner desire
For answers.
Where am I going?
What will I be doing?
A secret desire to succeed
Be really good at something successful.
Not daring to admit to another
A longing to be noticed
A little self worth and yes, importance.
Everyone has these moments of confusion
A lack of clarity
For you are not alone
Like so many.
Things will move
Scenarios will dampen your desire
But not forever.
There's a saying
Nothing is unachievable
The sky is the limit
Remember
The sky goes on further than your wildest dreams
And distances unattainable.
A little confusion can fire up creativity within
Observe, feel, digest and then go with it.

Star

You are a star
A star that shines so bright
A star that holds so many dimensions
Ricocheting light in all directions
Creating a little light to all.
Well, all that takes the time to notice
Become a little closer
Take the risk of discovering the unknown.
Stars are to be discovered
So many haven't been heard of or are unknown yet
But rest assured
True stars are always revealed to the world,
Just when the time is right.
A star will never go unnoticed
For it is impossible
To hide the love and light
That must be shared to others.
When the time is right
You will be guided
You will shine brightly
And there will be no stopping.
Once light is released
It creates, accumulates and spreads to all
Like all loving species.

Sounds

Wave upon wave of sounds
Vibrating through our universe and ourselves
Feel the vibration,
Not only listen but feel.
A song without any words
Is often far more powerful
As you listen and feel each note, vibration and emotion
Behind the fine tuning of the artist
Often inspired by an unexplainable desire to create music.
Where does the desire come from?
Very powerful creativity and born
With knowledge that has always been there.
Maybe born to inspire others
To help heal the wounded
Reignite creativity and thought provoking in all.
Truly listen, feel the vibrations all around you
The rustling of the leaves
You might notice a living creature habituating there.
Things you have never noticed before
We miss so much beauty within this earth plane
By not allowing ourselves the time or freedom
To use the gifts we were born to use and experience.
We are missing so much beauty across our land
Make that time to go back to basics
And you'll find you will lose that desire to compete with
materialism
For you will discover the greatest secret of all
IT TRULY MEANS NOTHING
You only borrow whilst you are here
You own nothing, but experiences.

Silence is Golden

Silence is golden
For some this is frightening
To be on one's own
To not be surrounded by others
The busy sound of chitter chatter
A multitude of emotions, drama and interaction
All feeding of one another's energy.
When does one explore or have time
To feel their own energy
How do you feel?
Very rare one asks another, how they feel
Even rarer you ask yourself how you feel.
It's good and healthy to have a little time on one's own
Time to reflect, clear your head
So you can enjoy the hustle and bustle of life.
But not to become so absorbed
In others anxieties, worries and concerns
You lose yourself in other's energies.
Always make time for yourself
So you can learn and develop
Watch others, never judge, learn
What is honourable and what is not
For you are an individual as are they
Never lose the art of being an individual
Silence is golden
Even if just for that.

A Kiss

It started with a kiss
A tender sweet kiss
I remember it well
He held my hand
Made me feel so special
Alive, vibrant, truly physically and mentally alive.
No insecurities
Just a sense of calm, belonging and very much loved
Throughout my life
I had you
So lucky.
For some aren't so fortunate
To experience a belonging, to be part of two
Which became a pack.
We protected our innocent
We nurtured, fed, clothed and watered
As best as we could
There were highs and lows
But we always knew we had each other.
The empowerment of knowing that we could take on the
world
Often we did, together.
Thank you for sharing my world and for being there
Every step of every minute of every hour, there for me.
I am truly blessed,
Thank you.

Believe

Believe, always believe in yourself
Never doubt why you are here
Why we are all here
We are here to make a difference
Not necessary to conquer the world
But make that difference.
Touch the heart of another
Lift another from the dark emotions of despair
A helping hand
A kind gesture
Never dampen or hide away from helping another
Or making excuses of
I haven't enough time
I don't want to get involved
You know when it is right to help another
As we were all born with the ability
To recognise a fellow human in times of difficulty.
To bury one's head in the sand
From reality of our surroundings and those in it
Is cruelty
Would you stand by and watch a wounded animal in despair
Even if there was nothing you could do?
Perhaps you would reassure the wounded animal by simply
being there.
The presence and strength of you
Hold the dog's paw, stroke the fur
Let them know everything's going to be alright
A calmness to give to a frightened other.
The final few minutes of the wounded animal's life
Feeling empowered
Safe and secure – NOT ALONE
Or perhaps bury your head in the sand?

Books

Sometimes open
Sometimes closed
Sometimes it remains on the same page
Unable to move on until finally read and understood.
Some books as people are complex
Some are so easy and fun to read,
Often a sad story will crop up
Some contain anger and hatred.
We are like libraries
Millions upon millions of different stories,
All waiting to be read, heard and understood.
But will another open the book
And try to understand the complex characters within
Or become bored and not complete the story?
Fascinating
Like books we all want time to be read
An emotional reaction
Any reaction is better than nothing.
Can we make another laugh,
Fill their life with a little light and good will
or will we inflict our emotions and distress on another?
Think
Just for a moment
How much responsibility we hold within the words we speak.
We all have so much responsibility
To pass words of encouragement and love on to another.
Next time you hear a horrendous story
From another that unnerves you
Maybe exchange it for a positive story instead
So to fill another's day with laughter and fun.
Just think of the impact you could create
With a happy story,

Especially if that person passes it on to another and then another
Perhaps a light library.
Thought provoking don't you think?

Tired

Tired
So many tired
Tired physically, some tired emotionally
So many so tired
Why?
Why so many tired?
We have so much
For most have a roof over their heads
Food in their stomachs
And clothes on their backs.
Tiredness comes from a lack of contentment
The wrong foods within our bodies
The stress and strains of striving
For objects of little meaning.
Tired of the cruelty of other's tongues
The little respect we give to each other
These things make you tired.
A mother's love gets her through the gruelling
Lack of sleep
For love is involved
As will your love for life get you through this chapter.
Some things are not worth becoming tired for
The top of the range car
The house with the extra bedroom
The holiday that will tire you out
For the next year, to pay for.
Life can be tiring
But not as tiring as we make it
Think
How can you unload your burdens?
Reduce the worry which is exhausting
In itself.
Stop, take reflection

And who knows you may become
Energized.

Shine On

Shine on, shine on
There may be troubles your way
Difficult times ahead
You know what is on your path
But you must
Shine on.
Let that light within shine brightly
Whatever is thrown at you
Throughout
You have no option but to
Shine on.
For others depend upon you
Your inner strength and jovialness,
If you don't shine
What light will they follow
To help them see through the dark?
They could become lost and falter off their path.
Shine on for there is no alternative
Apart from the depths of the dark.
Life is difficult, often draining
But also bright, joyous, fun and beautiful
So shine on for we need light everywhere.
Without light nothing can survive
Plants, vegetation, all living species
Will become no more.
Shine on.

Rejection

Rejection is not a nice feeling
Some can spend a lifetime of feeling rejected.
If made to feel like this constantly,
One will believe it.
If one believes it
Not are they only feeling rejected
But they start to reject others.
All goes full circle
What we give off to others,
That person will re-enact
See the circle of life.
For it takes the strong and bold
Courage
To break this circle
If another rejects you
Send them love and good health
For the circle will be broken
And no untoward will be able to manifest into your energy.
It is so important to spread circles of light and love to others
For this enables freedom and light
To touch the souls of many.
All by thoughts of encouragement and acts of acknowledging
others.
Always acknowledge a fellow human
A smile
A gesture
An acknowledgement that they are simply there.
Let's create the circle of love to all mankind
Who knows where it could lead to?
A content planet
Green spaces
Fresher air
The potential is endless.

Never reject another for the impact is astronomical.

Peace

Accept life for what it is
Strive to do well
To succeed
But don't forget to enjoy the journey.
Embrace the highs, the lows
The bumpy path
And acknowledge what you are learning
Also how you feel so differently
From one situation to the next.
Occasionally look back
See how far you have come
Especially emotionally and how you have grown.
Don't spend too much time looking backwards
As it is now, what matters
But it's healthy to reward your efforts
With a pat on the back from time to time.
Embrace the moment
Ask yourself how you feel today?
If the answer is rotten
Then ask yourself how you can change.
We have the ability to change circumstances in life
As we have all been given the keys to every door
It's just the decision in which one we will pick.
One of destruction or one of dismay and beauty
Never under estimate your ability to turn any situation around.
It's your path, your journey
One of peace if you allow
Or one of constant rushing and battles
I know which one I would pick
Don't you?

Trance

For a moment in time
Where were you?
You had escaped from the reality of the world
The hustle and the bustle.
Almost recharging one's batteries
Lost in time.
Sorry I was away with the …
Everyone needs to escape
Just for a few seconds
A quick break
An inner moment
Where it's just you and nothingness
Nothing to fear, nothingness
Actually quite beautiful
Pure
No corruption from outside views or influences
Just you
Beautiful, pure and vibrant
A vitality God or Divine
Stove upon you
That is the true you
Pure.

Sorcerer

Many people lost their fight for right to live
Over sorcery
Herbs of nature, cold and hot compresses of nothing
But herbs
That did heal.
Today more people are recognising the benefit of nature
And the effects on the body spirit and mind.
Many humans have been born
With the ability to heal
The subtlety of touch
The removal of unwanted energies
And stagnations surrounding one's energy.
How can that be physiologically possible?
No medical explanation
How?
Through a higher loving energy of course
Some things in life can't always be explained.
Miracles
Miracles are occurring every day
Throughout our world and beyond.
Not media driven as much as world wide
Disasters and evil occurrences.
Is this humans empowerment
Of controlling others by fear?
This has been a case throughout history
Dictated by varieties of leadership.
A repeated cycle
So who is the sorcerer?
Surely not the one who's
Creating miracles
Miracles of love?

Christmas

Christmas is the time to be jolly,
Really
Surely every minute of every hour of the day you should
rejoice,
For you are alive.
For many I hear – really
What is one to be jolly about?
Losing a loved one?
It's simple
You haven't
For they are truly a thought or merely a breath away.
Stop
Quiet your mind
Feel within
You already have an inner knowledge and understanding
For you, all of us are eternal souls.
Eternal souls
What does that mean?
We are an energy that can always evolve with time and
become greater with life experiences.
Happiness as well as sadness, pain and despair.
Through time you evolve and sadness becomes less.
Why is this?
Because each and every one of you are pure spirit,
The most beautiful pure energy as time evolves.
This is a cause of celebration not just for Christmas but every
day.
You are eternal
As so are your loved ones
And all will meet again for it is impossible not to.
So rejoice, wipe away tears for we are so close to our loved
ones
As I've already said – a heartbeat away.

Animals

Animals the purest gift of all
For what one sees one gets
Emotions so pure and honest
Love, unconditionally and without questioning,
No judgment of others
No ill acts of jealousy.
We can learn so much
If only one would stop and stare.
Look how grateful they are for
A pat or stroke, human contact.
See how content they are just to be near you.
So grateful for your time and presence
To be homed, fed and watered
That is all any of us really need.
But as animals
We, too, need to be acknowledged
Loved and nurtured to truly turn into a well-balanced
Whole person.
So stop and watch those animals
Often not appreciated by human folk and often by-passed
For they are very clever
For they have learnt the importance of this earth plane
Much quicker than us superior humans.
I question who is the superior creature them or us?

Corruption

So much corruption all around
Spiralling out of control
Wait a moment
Only if you allow it
Always see the beauty in your surroundings
Yes the atmosphere has been a little unsettled
But a lot of good work is being carried out to counteract.
The uncertainty of the current climate
So important for all to have fresh air
See the mountain tops covered in snow.
We weren't designed to relish and grow in concrete suburbs.
It will dampen one's soul
Cause all sorts of imbalances within
And unsettle the mind.
Some can afford to choose
Others can't
But always strive to be near Mother Nature.
It will settle the mind, body and soul
Vitally important
You must allow your inner self growth
And to do that you need to go back to basics.
Roam the raw elements of nature
Give yourself that, what has become a luxury
Fresh air.

Birds

Birds flying high in the sky
Roaming free
Gliding from different atmospheric winds.
Swooping low, flying high
Coasting in between
Not a care in the world.
The nest is ready
The home secure
Out of dangers way.
So now I can fly freely
Without a care in the world
For I have thought of others
I have tendered their needs
And now just for this moment
I FLY, FLY HIGH
Before the next gush of air sends me on my way.
For the lucky few to have watched their
Young grow safely out of harm's way
They have evolved
As nature intended
And fear nothing
A satisfaction and appreciation of one's life
The mighty fear nothing
For there is nothing to fear.
A passing from one world to simply another
FREEDOM.

Jealous, Angry and Sadness

A mixture of emotions
One minute jealous
That other, can't make the time for you
But the time is readily available for another
Why?
It's not for us to know why
But through your erratic emotions to accept.
Anger, a rush of rage deep within
Why?
Because you have lost control.
The lack of control a child feels
Remember
We are all children.
It's OK to feel like this
It shows the ability to care
Once again, you must show restraint.
Thirdly, here comes the sadness
The anger has worn you out
Now there is a welling of sadness
Plus a strong desire to cry.
Not nice
But once again you have to sense, feel and move on.
For the control of one's behaviour and actions are so powerful
But your ability to accept
The feeling, physically and mentally
Within are powerful, too.
Let the emotions flow
Embrace, digest and then let go
For if you do this, you will not pass on to another.
Experiences like these
Are not to be shared
They are to be learned from.
This is where you stop the cycle

The cycle of life must continue
But not the cycle of self hurt and emotional destruction within
You have to let it go.

Lion

The heart of a lion
A warrior who will not give up to the end.
A passion so strong to do what one knows is right
A beating heart of a drum
So strong it vibrates to all
For an inner strength and purpose to make a difference.
The heart and strength of a lion
They say the lion is king of the jungle.
So can you be
With that inner roar.
Although a lion is mighty
The lion must also provide
A safety for all those who surround and belong to the pride.
A strength that must be controlled
For if not tamed
The death, heartache and despair
Will be invoked to the surrounding pride
The impact on the food chain and nature astronomical.
So remember to roar with passion and good intention
But also with thought, integrity
And to benefit all
For you are the mighty lion
So go on roar.

Just for Today

Just for today smile
Inwardly smile and be thankful for all you have.
Just for today appreciate what you have
Don't look at what one hasn't got
But look at what you have got.
If it's just the clothes you are stood in then
Be thankful
For this provides you with warmth and protection.
So many haven't got the warmth and protection
Of clothing or family, let alone anyone they can turn to.
Pretty bleak really
Don't you think?
So just for today really look at what you have
And be thankful.

A Lost Lamb

You are not lost
You never were
Time will tell
All will be reunited
As two worlds merge into one.
On one side everything is seen so clearly
How one another feels
The emotions and burdens you have secretly hidden.
It's so easy to heal from our side
As everything is crystal clear
Every eventuality is explored
No hidden crevices to hide under
Pure, simple and honest.
First you have to be honest with yourself
Are you really lost?
Or have you created this?
Through turmoils of childhood memories of hurt and
insecurities
If you look a little deeper
Really look within
At another's perception of things
You'll find
You're not lost
Just confused by your feelings.
A little time is required
To reflect
Reverse roles and situations.
It's not always as simple as black and white
Open your heart to forgive
And to forgive yourself on your feelings
Created to others
Often horrid thoughts
Forgiveness to all

Stand back and observe
Observe with open eyes
Not partially open ones.

Home

A safe secure place
Freedom to be one's self
No inhibitions, no pretence
Just allowed to be one's self.
For the people around you except you for you
They know every fault and insecurity one possesses
But they don't care
For you are unique.
So special, only one of you that truly exists
Many similar
But only one you.
You must embrace this
Learn to really love yourself.
Be thankful for every experience thrown at you
It's how you deal with these occurrences, to how you learn
Not always the outcome
Always the process.
No one is rewarded by dark, unkind intentions
Only the light kind worker is acknowledged
As you will all discover with time.
If one crosses the line before another
But has done so with untoward actions or intentions
Send them love and wish them the best
For they have so much more to learn and discover.
Nothing in life goes unnoticed, it's the universal law.

Tarot

A mystical magical method designed
By monks hundreds of years ago.
A system devised by man once again
And tainted by ill wishers
Everything in life is judged by man
The positive review
Oh yes and always a negative review.
The tarot like all beliefs
Is tarred by sceptics and non believers
All beliefs can be beautiful and light
It depends upon the hands who handle such delicacies.
We have all heard and learnt about
Profits and saint-like humans
But also heard of the wounded young
Tainted by people of power and authority.
There will always be
Good and evil
For one must learn by unfortunate experiences
But remember
Light will always prevail
For light cannot be contained
Where there is hope and kindness
The light will infiltrate
And spread to every corner
Even the darkest of corners
For light fears nothing and only has
The desire to spread to all.
Never judge another's beliefs
Always remain non-judgmental.
Watch how that person conducts them self to all around
That is the true belief.
How you live your life
Honourably or wasted energy on judging others

Rather than living your life
And teaching others by your example.
Actions are louder than words
Especially when so many foolish
Preach to others
Live by example.

To Write

If only so many, would write
Write about their inner feelings
Aspirations, desires, fulfilling dreams,
What might feel silly to express to another
Or perhaps egotistical.
Who cares?
Just write
Write it down and who knows one day
It might become a reality.
A freedom with the pen to express yourself
Where words are almost forbidden
Write, express emotions
Allow your pen the freedom to roam
By this you are giving yourself
The freedom also.
Dreams do come true
Often helped by one expressing their thoughts.
Writing does not only allow freedom
But also a completion
Drawing a line in the sand.
Emotions put on paper have been expressed
Can now be set free.
Time to move on with other adventures
Allowing you the freedom to explore
And move on.
Not dragging unfinished business around with you
Attached to your back.
Write
And the load one carries on a daily basis
Will be lifted.
You will be lighter to gather new experiences through
Untainted eyes
The ability to see clearly.

A Leopard's Spots

What is the saying?
A leopard's spots will never change.
You cannot stop change
Everything moves on
For time stands still for no one.
It's how one changes
But surely that is up to you
Most grasp the lessons on their journey
Others are born wise souls
Almost as if they have been here before
Especially for some so wise and young.
Some will never learn from their mistakes
As they haven't the desire
And if being honest
Strive on little self worth
Often self destruction.
The choice is for each and every one of us
To evolve how we wish
Frustrating for so many
Especially the ones born to help the wounded souls.
We all have a purpose
Throughout our earthly time
Some will use it wisely
Other's not so
But one thing is for sure
You can change
A leopard can change its spots.

Cats

People often don't understand the cat
How creative and clever the cat is
When allowed the cat will allow you to stroke it
Knowing the importance and healing energy of its fur.
The calmness, contentment of exchange
Between owner, passer-by and animal
Cats sense when one needs a quiet moment
To connect with nature and the simplicity
A cat can give to another.
For affection isn't always given out freely
But when a fellow human has earn the trust
And proven themselves
To be worthy of affection and time.
Humans put themselves often on pedestals
Of greater intelligence compared to our four legged friends.
How many folk give their love so freely
To another that hasn't proved to be honourable?
So many end with burnt fingers
You never see a cat with burnt paws.
Too clever, yes, even for us humans.

Just a Thought Away

You were always there
By my side
My first steps of every kind
You were always there.
To have the love I've received
I'm truly blessed
Because you were always there.
Any doubts and troubled times
I always felt safe
That's because you were there
There was nothing in life
I couldn't overcome for there was
Always an answer, a solution
Because once again
You were always there.
Now you're gone
I feel all alone
But I know you will always be there
Until our paths meet again
I thank you
For always being there.

A Mother's Love

The most precious gift of all
A love that is unconditional, pure and honest
A protection
A desire to make everything safe, happy and balanced
A secure environment
A safe haven
Watch the lioness tentatively watching her cubs
Keeping them clean
Never allowing them to wonder out of sight
A bond so special
Almost magical
For there is no judgment or expectation.
A Mother only feels complete
When they see their young settled, happy and content
For then she has completed her vocation in life
And is pleased with herself
Yes it is OK for her to be pleased with herself
As she has nurtured to the best of her ability her young
Taught them what's right and wrong
Now it is up to them to be kind, caring and considerate to others.
Never devalue the role of a mother
Especially the self sacrifice
For those who take their role seriously
For they have put back more in society than the material earner.
They have put in LOVE.
Yes love
Back in society
Let's face it our society desperately
Needs a little more love.

Laughter

Laughter is so important
It heals the souls of all
The happiness and contentment
It's contagious.
If only one would lighten one's heart
Allow one's self to become that inner child
We could create more laughter
Which in return would create more joy.
Oh, the sound of true laughter
Fills the universe with light
All dark corners are unveiled
With the vibration of laughter
That darkness cannot exist.
For laughter in return creates love
Love is the power house of the planet and all within.
Some may mock others
For allowing one to be exposed,
To be ridiculed
But is this maybe an insecurity of another
Their inner desire to be free and to laugh.

To Be Humble

Always remain humble
Be humbled by life
The love of another
The clean air you breathe in
Be humbled by nature
And how much you have.
Never look at another's possessions
Be truly thankful for all you have
If you are blessed to be surrounded
By people who care and love you
Be thankful
For nothing in life should be taken for granted.
As the saying goes
Here today, gone tomorrow
Always be kind to everyone you meet
On your path
Also never take those on your journey for granted
People like all living species are precious.
To be surrounded by so many fellow folk is a luxury
For whole communities throughout history
Have been wiped out.
This is not fiction but fact
Be humbled by life
Never lose the ability to respect your fellow neighbour
For worldwide wars have proven this
Time and time again.
In war torn countries
The once annoying neighbour has gone
And one has found one's self alone
Without the comfort and support
Of a fellow human.
An existence of isolation,
The task of self survival by oneself.

Man wasn't designed to survive alone.
But to fight and survive for fellow humans
Part of a pack
Not alone.

Trust

Trust in yourself
Trust
Such a hard thing to do
For to truly trust takes a lot of courage
For those who learn how to trust themselves
Have the ability to conquer all.
Not just to achieve
But conquer.
Conquer their dreams and aspirations
On earth.
You have all been born for a special reason
Many simply to touch the soul of another
TRUST
All will be revealed
With patience, nurture and guidance
You will achieve
With trust you have the ability to conquer.
Always trust in yourself.

Cry

Yes, it is OK to cry
Let the tears roll freely from one's eyes
Express your hurt, pain and suffering
Let it all go
You must let it all go.
For tomorrow is another day
And the tear marks upon one's face might remain
But notice the tears have dried.
Eventually my love, the marks will also disappear.
But the memories will remain buried
Deep within.
We are so lucky to experience the power of love
To truly love another with all our heart
And to experience being loved in return.
To have been blessed with such
Is an honour
And such a special gift.
Once you have learnt the ability to love
It can never be taken away.
At times one might feel
I will never love again
But rest assured
You will
As we all will
For it is such a strong power.
LOVE.
It can't ever be contained
It will always break free
For no one can deny another that feeling
You are experiencing or once experienced.

A Pumping Heart

Feel the pumping heart
Pumping in perfect unison
Taken for granted
How amazing our bodies truly are.
Abused by so many
With substances
Whether that be too much
Caffeine, cake, cocaine or cigarettes
You get the picture.
Some abuse themselves with too much exercise
Another form of self harming
All inflicted on one's self
To compensate for a lack of love
Or insecurity.
We are all guilty
You might disagree
Oh yes, isn't that called denial?
It takes a strong person to identify one's weaknesses
But an even courageous person to act upon.
Place your hand upon your chest
Feel that amazing heart pumping
Maintaining your life.
Love who you are
Embrace every moment
And all the loved ones around
Even the people you find obnoxious
For they, like you
Are so precious
A ticking of time.

Blue Blue Skies

Look at the blue, blue skies
Not a cloud or a care to be seen
Because of the blue, blue skies
Something so pure about a clear blue sky
Tainted by nothing.
Just as you relax and enjoy the vision of baby blue
Such an innocent, fresh and crisp colour
A bird flies by and distracts you from the moment.
Then you notice trails of aircraft fumes
Nothing is how it appears in life
If you look a little deeper
Things and scenarios are evolving all the time.
What once was pure and how nature intended
Is fast becoming polluted
By fumes of manmade engineering.
Halt!
Where is that blue, blue sky?
It's in the mind
So why oh why?

Music

Music such a powerful gift
Can light a fire within the depths of darkness
Stir emotions deep within
To the depths of one's soul.
Setting hidden emotion, turmoils free from a sad soul
Can be reignited by the sound of music.
That chorus of beats, delicate tuning and vibrations
Stirs deep within
Allowing emotions to roam freely
Often emotions we didn't know we held within.
Music ignites passion, desire, expression and a sense of freedom.
Music is like a rainbow
All those beautiful colours
That captures your heart and allows you to explore your emotions.
It gives you permission to explore the emotions within
And allows that joyous expression
Powerful energy to run riot throughout every cell within your body
Allowed to be free out of control
Blissfully happy, just for those few moments
To be connected to your true inner self.
The one society or should I say ourselves hide
Listen to music
Sing along
Be happy
Be free.
Music such a powerful and healing gift
To be shared with all
Ignite that fire and beautiful soul within.

Poverty

So much poverty and desperation
Tears of desperation
A mother unable to feed and protect her young.
A diseased child, ill mother and dying father
Who will look after my remaining young?
Animal faeces floating in the water
One has to drink from
Praying for escapism
Desperate
Making pleas to God
I'll never be unkind to another as long as I live.
If only you will spare the life of …
No light
I can't see any light in all this darkness.
No love of life or any family remaining to care for
Or to be cared for
Poverty – True Poverty.
The loss of life, destruction of disease
The numb sensation within
No sparkle of hope held within one's eyes, poverty.
Don't shun away from your responsibilities
Help another in times of desperation
A prayer of positivity
If nothing else
To help another learn to feel
To feel anything is better than nothing.

Prayers

The sound of chanting
The tears of sadness
The joy of a safe arrival
We hear your prayers
Prayers that touch the souls of many.
The power of prayer
The healing energy passed from one another
Through prayer and kind intention.
For those who receive your prayers are blessed
For so many are forgotten
One mustn't worry about these people
For the energy created within
The power of your prayers
Reach many.
As we have mentioned before
We are all connected through strings of incomprehensible
systems of energy lines
All connected to one another
Perfectly timed and in unison
For there is no such thing as coincidence in life.
Every person you come into contact with is part of your journey.
Yes even for just a glance, or smile
We are all connected.
Your energy and theirs will entwine to help one another
And learn a greater understanding of mankind.

Hold Your Tongue

Just before you dive in
And add to the kerfuffle of erratic emotions,
Tainted with a sprinkle of anger and passion
Stop!
Say nothing and watch
The others work it out
Suddenly the once erratic emotions settle
Settle before your eyes
Why?
Because another hasn't fuelled the fire
The fire calms
And eventually settles.
It's possible the fire won't completely go out
But it's containable
If you care for another
Be passive and help them work it out rationally
For they will be so thankful
In the long run and will learn.
Or
You could fuel the fire
Which in turn will burn others
Possibly leave wounds
Or worse
Lifelong scars
Hold your tongue.

Respect

We spend such little time on the earth plane
So why bother at all?
So much confusion and so many lessons to learn
Again and again we see the same mistakes go around.
Why?
Because some are not ready to evolve and move on to the next
chapter.
We have to respect this
And never try to right the wrongs of others.
Each child is their own person within their own right
Even as an infant.
Yes we must guide, nurture and teach
What is right and wrong?
But never feel we have the right to dictate
Or live another's life for them.
As this is the cruellest act of all
Not to allow another to live one's life
So don't.
Guidance, nurture and lots of love are the keys
Nothing else
So simple but so hard to abide by.

Listen

Listen
One step at a time
Rome wasn't built in a day.
But that is no excuse
For one must strive at one's own pace
Never put off today what you can do tomorrow
For that is wrong.
So much wasted talent
Because they are waiting for that break.
It's a two way thing
Destiny and desire to succeed have to meet in the middle.
Those who truly succeed in life
Have a desire to make a difference
A real spark and light within.
Want to succeed
But also understand that nothing comes with ease and
standing by waiting.
You have talents, all of you
Some are gifted at helping others
Others are academics
We all have a purpose.
No time for self pity
Energy consuming and a wasteful sin.
You all have so much, time is precious
Use it wisely.
Instead of worrying what others might think,
Often they don't
Concentrate on what it is you are here to do
To achieve
To conquer
To make better and happier.
Anything positive is worth fighting and working hard for
Don't you agree?

Materialism

Funny how we compare one another on what we possess or own
Don't you think?
Hasn't that person done well in life?
With the huge house
The top of the range car
The clothes on their back.
Haven't they done well?
But have they?
I'm not saying all
But some have made a huge sacrifice.
For one might have lost the ability to see what truly matters.
One might have become so absorbed with what another has
They can't see through the fog and identify
What and how much they have.
Always striving for more and more
Living a life of material charades.
Often living beyond their financial ability
Seeing a lack of finance as failure.
An obsession that if not careful can become out of control
A whole life wasted on dissatisfaction on what they have.
Sad really
The real successful person in life is
The one who is capable to stop and stare.
Acknowledge the different seasons
How quick the changes occur in the young.
The food and taste on one's tongue
And the raw elements of the weather.
The warmth on one's skin
Whether that be from the sun or the comfort and warmth of one's home.
That's the true winner.
Time is of the essence

The presence of loved ones are to be treasured.
Nothing stands still for time
Here today, gone tomorrow
Materialism is a necessary but not an obligation.

So So Much

You all have so much
So so much
Look around you
So so much
Air to breath
If only so many would breathe properly.
For you as many
Breath from the ribs
Not even from the lower abdomen
Crazy
The simplicity of breathing
So many can't do
For stresses within society
And lack of greenery has
Suppressed and caused anxiety within
Creating a breathing method
Unnatural to man.
A baby expands its stomach
You can visually see
The little tummy expanding and deflating
How many adolescents and adults breathe properly?
As one becomes stressed and absorbed
By unnatural surroundings, media and social pressures
One forgets how to breathe properly.
So many have to relearn this natural gift
Through yoga, tai chi and other alternative methods
Usually because life has become too much.
Ill health and mental disease
Has made one re-evaluate life
What is important and what is not.
Taken back to basics
Spiralling out of control
A flicker within

Saying
NO MORE
I want simplicity
Not self-consumed anxiety and misery
But simplicity
One of self discovery
An inner desire
To embrace who you really are
Not one of
Who you are supposed to be
Or created by a society of self-proclaimed know it alls.
The journey of self sabotage
And unbeknown to you
Negativity.
Through you and your inner self
You have the choice to reclaim.
Time to rejoice
For now you can be true to yourself
Who you are
What is right and wrong?
See and have the ability to visualise and yes, create
Not only a life of self worth
But one of breath
To breathe again.

Treasure

Gold, silver, flash cars
Houses of such obscenity, need I go on?
How much wealth does one need, really need?
So many want so much
Such greed and little understanding of what is important.
A home is a place that feels safe and warm
The people make the home
The heart of the family
Usually consists of a person
Not bricks and mortar.
The welcoming smile and an almost
Immediate feeling of acceptance,
A place where you can be open
To all and not worried about upsetting another.
This simplicity is called treasure
For so many are alone and suffering
From mental disease and low self esteem
Surrounded by the finery we all desire
Surrounded by towers of self preservation, isolation and misery.
A building often so grotesque
The family don't communicate
And neither have a desire to
Not even truly knowing one another
Or how and what makes that person tick.
It's called the unnoticed generation
The young submerged in technology
A world of false imaginary and fantasy
Trapped in a world
I suppose you could say
The matrix.

Value

Value everything around you
Value the view from your window
Whatever view you see.
Take it in, really look and notice
Each time you look you will notice something different.
Amazing how much goes unnoticed
Even sadder how many people go unnoticed.
Life is precious for we are here to learn
And make a difference
Whatever that difference is
You will all make a difference.
For the energy of your footprints always remain
Remain in another's thought
Touched another's soul
Held dear to another's heart.
Everyone is to be valued
Even the unpleasantness we will experience.
For these are valuable lessons
That makes us who we are
And enable us to value another and to be valued.
So please value
Value everything
Whether negative or positive
Throughout life
Value.

A Ring

A ring: a symbol of commitment
Beholding your love to another.
A friendship ring
Or just a statement of wealth and opulence.
A ring
A piece or silver, gold, diamonds, precious stones
Really quite funny how we show our love
By material gestures.
How about a cup of tea
So many craving for human contact
A hug?
A hug – if meant,
Says so much and heals so many
And often silent without words
Can be so powerful.
It may allow another the freedom to crumble
Knowing they are safe in the arms of another,
Knowing they will not fall
Precious, a hug
More precious than any precious stone I can think of
Don't you think?

Don't Worry

Don't worry my child
For I am by your side
Every step you take
I will be watching.
Not only watching
But guiding
Guiding to make the path clear for you.
We all have a path throughout life
That one must face and travel
At times it may appear alone
But let me tell you my child
You are never truly alone.
No one walks the path of life alone
Many a guide may go unnoticed
But very rarely completely unnoticed
For every one of you
Walks the path with many
For these are called your guides or guardian angels.
Angels from above
These beautiful light workers
Are here to assist you.
So many we hear laugh
Please do laugh
For true laughter is healing.
But we hear not true laughter
We hear false laughter
As the person's subconscious is aware
Like you are all aware
But just a topic not to be spoken of by so many.
If one wants to know the truth
ASK!
Ask the above and you will be shown.

Learn

Time is of the essence
So many times we repeat this statement.
Time is of the essence
You must do today what is right for today
If you have a thought or concern for another
Act on it today.
Today is the here and now
Tomorrow may never occur
You must all live in the here and now.
Not tomorrow, next week, next month, next year
NOW!
Something keeps reminding you of another
That person or situation keeps occurring within your thoughts
Now act upon that feeling
Never question your inner self.
We hear so many
I was just going to
Why didn't I listen to myself?
The time has come for all to learn
The act of listening to one's self.
It's not something new you have to learn
You were born with this ability
But for some reason you chose to unlearn it
It's time to learn.

Someone Special

Some are born in life
With something a little extra special about them
An unexplainable spark
A spark invisible to the eye
But such a special something
It draws people in
A light
That ignites and attracts all.
A wanting for others, to spend time with
Allowing a freedom for others to talk
To be honest and not hold back.
Why?
Because this person is non judgmental
Safe and kind.
You know your words will never touch another's ears
This person is so special
They are open, honest and funny
Truly alive
They make everyone feel noticed and important.
That's what makes this person shine
In fact almost angel like
Although this person would laugh at this comment
But it's true.
Thank you.

The Power of the Pen

A pen can be used for creativity
Encouragement and words of endearment
A little effort and thought with a pen can be life changing.
To know someone is thinking of you
And has gone to the effort of letting you know
So personal putting pen to paper
For each one of us has unique handwriting
That tells a story
Of one's personality.
It's so important we don't lose the art of writing
Just typing
For we will lose that human touch
And deeper integrity.
A little effort with a pen
Is so powerful
Of course
If used in light and jest.
Another responsibility to make that time
To write.

Let it Flow

Stop
Look at the picturesque water fall
Surrounded by flora and fauna
The beautiful colours
Merging into one another
The reflection of the light
Playing tricks with one's mind.
Beauty is in the eye of the beholder
What one feels and sees as beauty
May repulse another
What one might find endearing and loving
Might horrify another
We all see things so different
Not always quite to that extreme
But subtle and often miniscule
Always with a slight difference.
Nothing is black and white
Everything is unique.
You might see a stone
Another might see moss growing upon it resembling life.
One might see a horrid, foul self-centred individual
Another might see a wounded, insecure child hidden within.
One might see a serious academic miserable
Uptight person.
Another might see a person who cares
So deeply about our world with a desire to make it better.
RESPECT
Don't try and fathom another
Just accept and respect, we are all unique.
More to the eye
Than what one can physically see.

Be Excited

Be excited by life
Every corner you turn
Every crevice you discover
Life is so exciting
For one truly never knows what to expect
But expect you must
For time stands still for no one.
Everything evolves at great rates.
Grab every opportunity that comes your way
If it excites you and feels right.
For life is for living
As living is part of life
So much to learn, teach and share with others
Even if just your experiences.
So yes excitement about life is good
For life can be exciting.

Clarity

Just for today
Have clarity
Listen to others and hear their anxiety and concerns.
It's not coincidental
You have been experiencing the same thoughts and worries
You are being taught all the time
It's whether your ears are ready to receive
Your heart is open
And your mind receptive.
Just for today
You will receive clarity
Funny how your inhibitions and deepest thoughts will be made clear.
As we have said
There are no such things as coincidences.
An open mind, uncluttered
A willingness to listen
To another's concerns.
Another will answer your concerns
And answer their own at the same time
Clarity will occur
Clarity is all around waiting to be received
Waiting patiently to be accepted
Clarity.

Listen to the Children

Listen to the untainted children
The innocent
The clarity in the words they speak
The honesty and integrity they process
Where did all that goodness come from?
What has made them often so wise and organic?
How they view the world?
A world of so much beauty and simplicity
Light and dark
Right and wrong
Good and bad.
It's quite simple really
No need to analyse
Dissect and re-evaluate.
It's either honourable or kind or not?
We can all change our views and opinions to suit
What we want to hear and justify
For our own benefit
Or to justify our actions
And yes of course, our beliefs
But everything is straight in front of us.
We can see what is right and wrong
Surely?
Or maybe one doesn't want to
It might upset us and others
The truth.
Unfortunately the truth and light
Will always prevail
For nothing can be hidden forever
Light and goodness
Cannot be contained
Where there is a gap in one's life
The light will find a way to stream out

Free
All will see the truth once again
Through the eyes of the children.

Self-Acceptance

Self acceptance
So difficult for so many
So self critical of ourselves and yes sad to say others.
As a child you self accept
You love your body
It's all so marvellous each finger and toe
And your tummy fascinates you especially
That wonderful tummy button in the middle.
How lucky you feel to have one the same as others.
Then as time goes on
The imperfections start
Someone makes an innocent comment
Oh goodness look at the size of that tummy
You look as though you'll pop.
Then the comments become fast and furious from others.
These others have usually been bombarded with the same
vocabulary
And haven't learnt the art of self acceptance.
Sad how we inflict our insecurities on others.
Especially to the young who are born
With such self acceptance.
Thought provoking, don't you think?
So here's a challenge
Look at yourself, scars and all
And love every ounce of yourself.
Also what's inside this amazing shell that allows you to live?
Yes, the you inside
That perfect soul that's alight within.

Always Stay True to Yourself

Always stay true to yourself
When all around is evolving, opportunities arising
Maybe fortunate to experience the finery of life
Well materially
Don't succumb to the demands and expectations
Of those who suddenly surround you.
Remember your upbringing
Also, the kind words and teachings
The important words spoken by your parents
Always do your best and be kind to others.
You can never falter off your path
If you abide by this simple statement
To do your best involves being the best you can
Thinking of others and remaining humble,
Values of kindness will enable you to see clearly
Look and learn of the reactions you receive in return.
You will surround yourself with like-minded people
Who one can trust
As the saying goes, like attracts like
So never fear the path you take in life
For there is nothing to fear
If one stays true to one's self.

Pastures Green

As one leaves this world
Another is born
This is the cycle of life.
Grief stricken, heart wrenching pain of losing the one so dear
You know within they haven't gone far
But long so much for the warmth and touch of the flesh.
With time the hurt will settle
But the memories will always remain within
Life can often seem cruel
Although this is not intended.
We all have individual lives to live
Some will have sadder stories to tell
But all will be reunited for that is inevitable
As we will all experience the loss of another
No one escapes this tragedy
If you have experienced the despair of losing a loved one
Only you will be able to empathise
And feel the hurt of another.
You just being there for another will be healing in itself.

Feelings

Feelings of physical
Feelings of emotions
Feelings that are unexplainable
Feelings are such beautiful, powerful tools
We all possess
But unfortunately far too often ignored
Or I'm sad to say suppressed.
A knowing of an occurrence before it occurs
A funny feeling within
A heart wretched concern of an impending happening
A knowing there is nothing you can do to stop
Or control the occurrence.
Powerful us humans
Just how nature evolved with us working alongside it
Many a moon ago.
Now we work against it
Strange how we have evolved
Or
Not evolved
For now if we had evolved how nature intended
We wouldn't have as much
Mental disease
And we would understand our inner feelings and emotions.
We would have learnt the art of self expression,
Better communication,
An understanding of our fellow humans
Psychological needs and imperfections.
Learnt to put a greater importance
On integrity towards one another and felt, sensed and knew
How to help one another.
Never mind
Where there is hope there is will

And whilst there is will and desire to help other fellow humans
There is HOPE.

Christmas Memories

Holly and berries
Mistletoe and wine
Laughter and joy
But also a time to reflect
Reflect and enjoy
Memories are to be treasured
The good, the bad, the indifferent
It's how you interpret memories.
Memories are precious,
Be thankful for all the wonderful times,
Happy moments of laughter and joy.
Feel that love and laughter
It's still there
All you have to do
Is sit quietly and remember
For nothing has changed
A breath away
A flicker of light
All will be reunited again.
But for now remember
By this, one mustn't dwell
For that offends our loved ones.
Laugh, love and rejoice with them
For they feel your love
And if you try, you can also feel their presence.

Happiness (Children)

Hear the laughter of the children
Playing together
The deep joyous chuckle within.
Allowing free expression from deep within
Beautiful, care free and pure.
The energy of joy
Can light up the room
It's contagious; it lifts a spark within ones soul
And makes you feel blissfully happy.
So powerful children
Yet so often by-passed and not given enough time and
appreciated.
Always encourage laughter and fun within the young
For these special little people are, our future
The future of our planet.
Suppress the light-hearted
The world will become grey
Nurture, guide and teach our young
Our world will become full of ripeness and plantation
Where who knows, one could live in harmony.
Look at the young
See the fire lit brightly in each child.
Never dampen that light
For we need light within our world
As we all know without the sun
Earth cannot survive.

Serenity

Green rolling hills of green grass
Beautiful meadows
Wild flowers
Why they are called wild, I don't know
Organic and truly beautiful
For they haven't been engineered or tampered with
Pure, how nature intended.
Smell the fresh air, so subtle
Yet can reduce one to speechlessness
For all those delicate fragrances
Have become and are becoming such a rarity.
So much of our planet is becoming man made
Tampered with
Not how Mother Nature or the loving Divine
God, if that's your belief intended.
As religion, time, history has always preoccupied.
Forget the above, let's keep it simplified
MAN has the freedom to work with or against nature.
The latter at the moment
I am saddened to say
When will mankind acknowledge
The destruction he holds within his hands?
When it is too late
When we hear the chainsaw erupt with the final cutting of the
tree
When?
I hear your thoughts
How can we stop this?
If we all did a little just by planting a few seeds
Allowing Mother Nature to roam her land
The animals and insects will do the rest.
They need plantation and vegetation to survive.
To keep the cycle alive

And in return us alive.
So plant flowers and create more greenery
Even if it's just in one's back garden.
Mother Nature needs us
As we need Mother Nature.

The Powerhouse is Love

Love
The powerhouse of the universe
A word that expresses such beautiful
And heartfelt emotions.
Love, it leaves you speechless
For the feeling
Ignites such fulfilment, contentment and happiness.
There are so many different forms of love
The love of a child
Is different to one of a partner
This is different to one of nature, food,
The air we often take for granted.
Pure love is all of the above and more.
A knowing, sensing, feeling and being
The powerhouse of life and beyond
Love.

Fear

Fear and anxiety, what are these?
Manifested deep within
Emotions in turmoil spiralling out of control.
Wait a minute, who has control?
You
Settle my child for this is self-created.
Easier said than done, I hear so many times
But it's true
Embrace these emotions as this assures one's self
You are alive.
Let the adrenaline pump around one's body
But stop
Quiet one's self
It's all manifested from within
Hear the beat of your heart
The tremble within.
You are truly alive
Calm your mind
Breathe deep within
Change that energy to vitality
For all to share and admire.
Give that spark of life to another.
Another might have lost that desire
Lost the ability
To feel that adrenaline
And no longer feel alive.
Give that spark of energy freely.
Reignite that darkness within the sorrow of a soul
And embrace every moment.
For some aren't as lucky as you
To have the ability to feel emotion
For they didn't embrace
The flicker once held within.

Don't become one of many
Always be and feel alive.
To feel is better than to be empty.

Anger

Anger, hatred, despair
Manifesting, spiralling out of control
Yes out of control
So so wrong
The next feeling you will experience
Is one of disappointment
Did I really just behave like that?
Yes you did
We must all express our feelings
But it is how you express it,
Isn't it?
Control and ownership are forms of expression too
If you are in control of yourself
And take ownership for your behaviour
You will also experience
Empowerment and reward
You will reap the rewards of life
And life will be rewarded.
You manifest energy to others and they
Learn from you and re-enact.
Frightening how powerful we humans are
And how we can create
Light or dark energy through ones behaviour
Self-control is the answer
Ownership
Always take ownership for your behaviour
And never allow a situation
To manifest from lack of control
This is very important.

Born Again

You are born again
I hear so many
You can choose again and again how many times
You are born again.
You, like so many have the ability
To wipe the slate clean
And begin again.
So many dwell in the past
Over unkind and often evil occurrences
Especially through the eyes of a child
Children see occurrences through simplicity
What was wrong was wrong
No judgement of or complication
Either right or wrong.
One must acknowledge these memories
Allow them to run their course.
Don't stop the memory mid way
Or it will reoccur over and over again
Remember digest, hurt, scream and shout
If that's what it takes
To begin the healing process within
Then you must shine
Shine on.
For your strength and ability to shine through adversity
Will empower so many
Everywhere you walk through life
Your energy will help another
Without you even being aware
Reignite and yes allow others to start afresh
And become like you and many others
Re-born.

A Compass

A North, East, South and West divide
Apparently
Who stumbled upon this theory?
Oh yes,
Like all beliefs and manmade nonsense.
MAN!
There is no divide for we are all one
When you get to know another
You will see elements of that person in you
Like a mirror reflection.
A person you find unkind and often obnoxious
If you look a little deeper
The reason you don't like that person
Is because you can see yourself in that person
And they are bringing those dislikes about you to the surface.
They are there to remind you
You too are capable
And often behave in an unappealing way.
It makes you shudder because you know
That person is a part of you.
We meet people for a reason
Even if just to remind us how far we have come
Not to take anything for granted.
For we all have free will and it doesn't take much
To slide in the wrong direction
But thankfully also in the right direction.
Be careful how you view the world
Always see the beauty and good in all
Although hard at times
For this will enable you to see more clearly
The beauty in you.